D0301093

Lancashire Library Services	
30118134755929	
PETERS	J938GLO
£4.99	09-Jun-2017
EBA	

It's all about...

GLORIOUS GRÊEKS

KINGFISHER

First published 2017 by Kingfisher
An imprint of Macmillan Children's Books
20 New Wharf Road, London N1 9RR
Associated companies throughout the world
www.panmacmillan.com

Series editor: Sarah Snashall
Series design: Anthony Hannant (LittleRedAnt)
Written by Sarah Snashall

ISBN 978-0-7534-3936-4

Copyright © Macmillan Publishers International Ltd 2017

All rights reserved. No part of this publication may
be reproduced, stored in or introduced into a retrieval
system, or transmitted, in any form or by any means
(electronic, mechanical, photocopying, recording or
otherwise), without the prior written permission of
the publisher. Any person who does any unauthorized
act in relation to this publication may be liable to
criminal prosecution and civil claims for damages.

9 8 7 6 5 4 3 2 1

1TR/0916/WKT/UG/128MA

A CIP catalogue record for this book is available from the British Library.

Printed in China

This book is sold subject to the condition that it shall not, by way of trade
or otherwise, be lent, resold, hired out, or otherwise circulated without the
publisher's prior consent in any form of binding or cover other than that
in which it is published and without a similar condition including this
condition being imposed on the subsequent purchaser.

Picture credits
The Publisher would like to thank the following for permission to reproduce their material.
Top = t; Bottom = b; Centre = c; Left = l; Right = r
Cover iStock/Tolga TEZCAN; pages 2–3, 30–31 iStock/Sergey Borisov; 4 Kingfisher Artbank;
5 Shutterstock/elgreko; 5t Bridgeman/Look and Learn/Private Collection; 6 Alamy/Art Archive;
7 Kingfisher Artbank; 7t Shutterstock/Ksenija Toyechkina; 8 Shutterstock/Havoc; 9 iStock/
mladn61; 9t Flickr/Xuan Che; 9c Alamy/Classic Image; 10 Alamy/Art Archive; 11t Shutterstock/
Ivelin Radkov; 11tr Shutterstock/kamira; 11b Kingfisher Artbank; 12 Shutterstock/Anastasios71;
13 Shutterstock/Lambros Kazan; 13t Shutterstock/Gilmanshin; 14–15b Kingfisher Artbank;
15 Shutterstock/WitR; 16 Alamy/Steve Whyte; 17 Alamy/Heritage Image Partnership; 17b AKG/
Erich Lessing; 18, 19, 20 Kingfisher Artbank; 19t Shutterstock/arka38; 21 Alamy/epa european
pressphoto agency; 21t Shutterstock/Tatiana Popova; 22 Alamy/Prisma Archivo; 23t iStock/
kwanisik; 23b Shutterstock/Everett; 24 iStock/alxpin; 24b Kingfisher Artbank; 25 Alamy/age
fotostock; 25c Alamy/Prisma Archivo; 26 Alamy/Active Museum; 26–27 Kingfisher Artbank;
27 Shutterstock/Gilmanshin; 28 Shutterstock/Everett; 29t Shutterstock/Firdea Saylian;
29 Alamy/robertharding.
Cards: front tl Alamy/Mary Evan Picture Library; tr iStock/fotofojanini; bl Museumsber
Flensburg/Axelv; br Rowanwindwhistler; back tr Kingfisher Artbank; bl Flickr/Xuan Che;
br iStock/vukkostic.

Front cover: Ancient mosaics in the city of Antakya (called Antioch in ancient times)
in modern Turkey.

CONTENTS

For your free audio download go to
http://panmacmillan.com/gloriousgreeks
or goo.gl/luufGL
Happy listening!

People of Ancient Greece

The Ancient Greeks lived in and near Greece about 2500 years ago. They did not belong to one country but to a number of separate city states, which shared a similar culture and language.

The people of Ancient Greece lived on the mainland as well as on islands dotted around the Aegean Sea.

Mount Olympus

Troy

Greece

Athens

AEGEAN SEA

Olympia

Cyclades

Sparta

SEA OF CRETE

Knossos

MEDITERRANEAN SEA

Crete

4

We remember the Greeks for their learning, plays, myths and gods, pottery, games and temples.

SPOTLIGHT: Archimedes

Dates: 287BCE – 212BCE
Occupation: mathematician and inventor
Famous for: Archimedes screw
Quote: 'Eureka!' (I've found it!)

Many Ancient Greek ruins can be seen today.

The king and the monster

The first Greek civilization was on the island of Crete. Legend says that King Minos lived in the palace of Knossos in Crete, and that under his palace was a labyrinth. A half-man, half-bull monster called the Minotaur lived in the labyrinth.

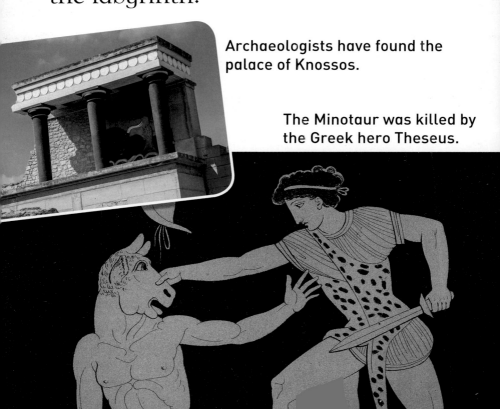

Archaeologists have found the palace of Knossos.

The Minotaur was killed by the Greek hero Theseus.

At festivals in Knossos, acrobats used to leap across the horns of a bull.

FACT...

A Greek legend says the people of Athens had to send seven boys and seven girls each year to feed the Minotaur.

The Trojan War

The poet Homer told how, in the time of heroes, Greeks attacked the city of Troy (in modern Turkey). After ten years, the Greeks pretended to sail away, leaving a wooden horse behind. The Trojans took the horse inside the city, but it was a trick! The horse was filled with Greek soldiers.

The Greek hero Achilles fought outside the walls of Troy.

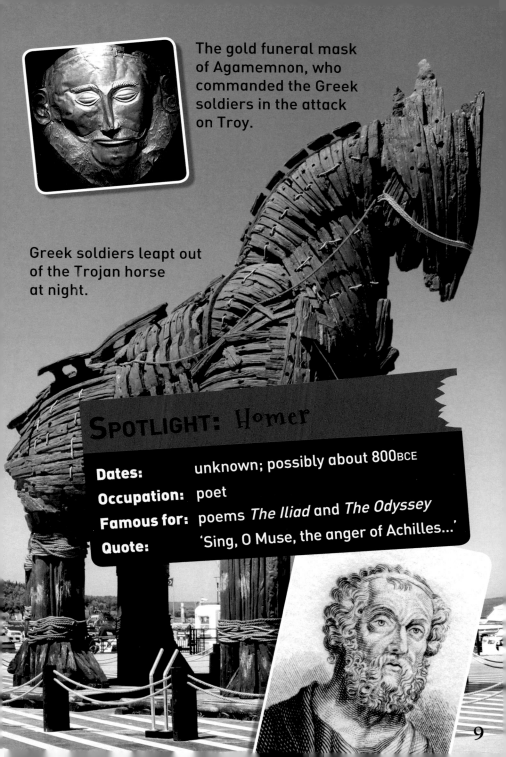

The gold funeral mask of Agamemnon, who commanded the Greek soldiers in the attack on Troy.

Greek soldiers leapt out of the Trojan horse at night.

SPOTLIGHT: Homer

Dates:	unknown; possibly about 800BCE
Occupation:	poet
Famous for:	poems *The Iliad* and *The Odyssey*
Quote:	'Sing, O Muse, the anger of Achilles...'

9

Traders and settlers

The Ancient Greeks lived in cities along the coast and on islands. These cities ruled themselves, traded around the Aegean Sea and became very rich. Greek traders and farmers began to create their own settlements in Italy, Spain, Africa and Turkey.

Many Greeks became rich enough to own expensive jewellery.

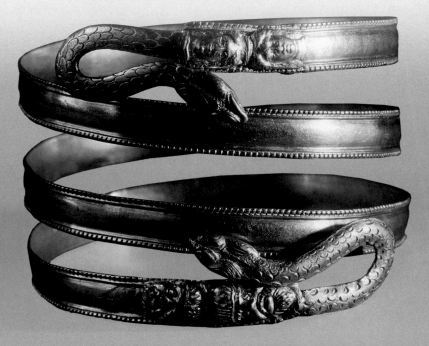

The Greeks created beautiful decorated pots.

The Ancient Greeks used gold and silver coins. City states had their own coin designs.

FACT...

A Greek colony abroad kept links to its 'mother city' (*metropolis*, in Greek).

Traders used ships with oars and sails to trade across the sea.

Athens versus Sparta

The two most important city states were Athens and Sparta. Athens was the centre of arts and learning. Sparta was a warrior state where boys left home to join the army at five years old. Athens had powerful warships; Spartans had the strongest army.

FACT...

Spartan children were taught not to cry.

Leonidas was one of the most famous kings of Sparta.

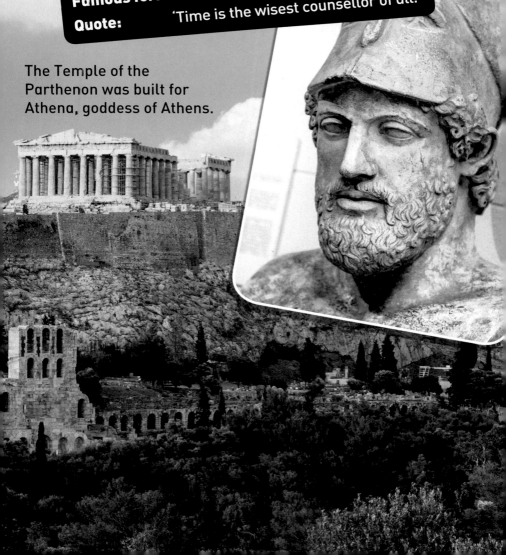

SPOTLIGHT: Pericles

Dates:	495BCE – 429BCE
Occupation:	general and leader of Athens
Famous for:	making Athens great
Quote:	'Time is the wisest counsellor of all.'

The Temple of the Parthenon was built for Athena, goddess of Athens.

Gods and goddesses

The Ancient Greeks worshipped a family of gods who lived on Mount Olympus. Each god looked after a different area of life. The gods could walk on the Earth and help, punish or even fall in love with humans.

Zeus was the king of the gods.

Aphrodite was the goddess of love.

Athena was the goddess of wisdom.

The temple at Cape Sounion was dedicated to Poseidon, god of the sea.

FACT...

Athena, the goddess of wisdom, was cut from the head of her father Zeus. She was fully grown and dressed in armour.

Heroes and monsters

The Greeks told stories – myths – about their gods. They also told stories about monsters, bad kings and heroes. Polyphemus was a one-eyed giant who lived on an island. King Midas foolishly wished that everything he touched would turn to gold. The hero Jason fought a snake to capture a golden fleece.

Perseus killed the snake-headed Gorgon, called Medusa.

Icarus had wings of wax and feathers, made by his father. Icarus flew too close to the Sun, his wings melted and he fell into the sea.

The Greek hero Heracles (below) carried out twelve impossible tasks.

FACT...

In one myth, a woman called Arachne claims to be a better weaver than Athena, so Athena turns her into a spider.

17

Greeks at war

The Greek city states often fought against each other. But when invaders came from Persia, the city states fought together against their common enemy.

Soldiers wore a helmet, tunic, breastplate and greaves (leg protectors).

The most important soldiers were foot soldiers called hoplites. They fought in a combined team called a phalanx.

Each hoplite carried a long spear and a shield.

The trireme was a fast battleship rowed by 170 oarsmen arranged in three rows.

Olympic Games

Once every four years a truce would be held between the fighting city states so that everyone could travel safely to the Olympic Games in Olympia. These were the most important of the four athletic games of Ancient Greece and were held in honour of Zeus.

Athletes would compete in discus throwing, running, javelin throwing, long jump and wrestling.

The stadium at Delphi was used for the Pythian Games.

FACT...

The first known Olympic champion
was a baker called Coroebus in 776BCE.

A torch-lighting ceremony for the modern
Olympic Games is held at the site of Ancient Olympia.

Clever Greeks

The Ancient Greeks had a great respect for learning and for discussing ideas. They were very interested in talking about maths, science, medicine, politics and the meaning of love and life. Many of these Greek thinkers are still famous today.

Socrates was one of the first and most important philosophers, but his ideas scared some people.

FACT...

Hippocrates studied medicine at a healing temple on the Greek island of Kos. He is known as the 'father of Western medicine'.

ruins of temple on Kos

Famous Greek thinkers

Socrates	philosopher
Plato	philosopher
Aristotle	philosopher
Hippocrates	doctor
Archimedes	scientist
Pythagoras	mathematician

Pythagoras believed maths would help us to understand the world.

Theatres and festivals

Poetry, music, storytelling and theatre were important in everyday life and in religious festivals in Ancient Greece. The festival in Athens of Dionysos, the god of wine, included drama competitions.

FACT...

Sophocles was the first playwright to use stage scenery.

The theatre at Epidauros could hold 14,000 people.

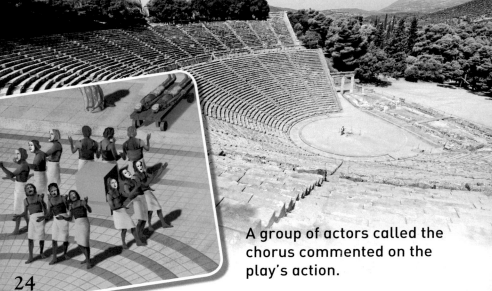

A group of actors called the chorus commented on the play's action.

The plays were either happy, funny or romantic comedies, or serious tragedies.

The actors (all men) wore masks to show the character they were playing.

SPOTLIGHT: Sophocles

Dates:	about 497BCE – about 405BCE
Occupation:	playwright
Famous for:	plays *Oedipus* and *Antigone*
Quote:	'... no success without hardship.'

Everyday life

People in Ancient Greece wore simple clothes made of linen or wool and pinned at the shoulder. Richer Greeks might also wear a richly coloured cloak fastened with a brooch or pin. Slaves wore short tunics and no shoes.

Women wore a sleeveless tunic with a high belt.

Greek houses had a courtyard in the centre, light-coloured walls, and tiled roofs and floors to keep the rooms cool.

Women sometimes wore elaborate hair-styles.

The houses of wealthy Greek families had a separate area where the women could weave.

Alexander the Great

The last great leader of Ancient Greece was Alexander the Great. When he was 20 years old, Alexander became king of Macedonia – the most powerful Greek state at the time. He wanted to create an empire for Greece. First he attacked and defeated the Persian Empire, then he invaded countries farther east.

Alexander fought the Persian Emperor, Darius.

8

FACT...

Alexander was taught by the great philosopher Aristotle.

SPOTLIGHT: Alexander the Great

Dates:	356BCE – 323BCE
Occupation:	king and conqueror
Famous for:	defeat of Persia
Quote:	'Every light is not the sun.'

The ruins of a temple built by the Ancient Greeks in Failaka (modern Kuwait).

GLOSSARY

Aegean Sea The sea that lies between Greece (to the west) and Turkey (to the east).

BCE Short for 'Before the Common Era' (any date before 1CE). It is also sometimes known as BC (before Christ).

city state A city and the area around it that rules itself.

colony A group of people from one country who live together in another country.

courtyard An open-air area with walls.

culture The ideas, art and customs of a group of people.

invaders People who try to take over a place by force.

labyrinth A maze.

legend A traditional tale that might be based on an original true story.

mainland The large part of a country; the opposite of an island.

mortal A living human being; the opposite of a god.

philosopher Someone who studies and thinks about knowledge, truth and the meaning of life.

playwright Someone who writes plays.

protector Someone who looks after something or someone.

settlements Places where people settle down to live and create a small village or town.

temple A building in which people worship a god or goddess.

trader A person who buys goods and sells them to someone else in order to make money.

truce A time when two enemies decide to stop fighting.

tunic A short, sleeveless dress.

weaver Someone who makes cloth.

INDEX

Collect all the titles in this series!

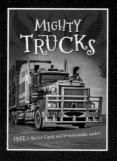
BEASTLY BUGS
FREE Collector Cards and Downloadable Audio!

DEADLY DINOSAURS
FREE Collector Cards and Downloadable Audio!

EPIC EXPLORERS
FREE Collector Cards and Downloadable Audio!

EXOTIC EGYPTIANS
FREE Collector Cards and Downloadable Audio!

FANTASTIC FLIERS
FREE Collector Cards and Downloadable Audio!

FAST CARS
FREE Collector Cards and Downloadable Audio!

FREEZING POLES
FREE Collector Cards and Downloadable Audio!

GLORIOUS GREEKS
FREE Collector Cards and Downloadable Audio!

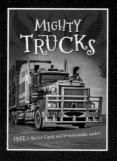

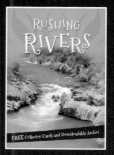

MIGHTY TRUCKS
FREE Collector Cards and Downloadable Audio!

REMARKABLE ROMANS
FREE Collector Cards and Downloadable Audio!

RIOTOUS RAINFOREST
FREE Collector Cards and Downloadable Audio!

RUSHING RIVERS
FREE Collector Cards and Downloadable Audio!

GLORIOUS GREEKS

Collector Card

GLORIOUS GREEKS

Collector Card

GLORIOUS GREEKS

Collector Card

GLORIOUS GREEKS

Collector Card

Polyphemus

A nasty one-eyed man-eating giant who tried to capture Odysseus.

SCORE

STRENGTH:	9
CLEVERNESS:	2
BRAVERY:	5
FAMILY: son of Poseidon	9

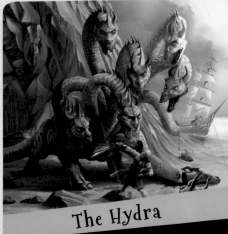

The Hydra

A monstrous multi-headed serpent that was defeated by Heracles.

SCORE

STRENGTH:	5
CLEVERNESS:	4
BRAVERY:	6
FAMILY: grandson of Gaia and Tartarus	4

The Sphinx

A part-lion, part-eagle, part-woman monster defeated by Oedipus.

SCORE

STRENGTH:	4
CLEVERNESS:	8
BRAVERY:	3
FAMILY: daughter of Echidna	5

Cerberus

The three-headed guard dog of the Underworld who ate living people.

SCORE

STRENGTH:	3
CLEVERNESS:	3
BRAVERY:	3
FAMILY: son of Echidna and Typhon	5